ABRAHAM LINCOLN

by Anna Sproule

Picture Credits

Associated Press — 59; The Bettmann Archive — 16-17, 29, 46 (lower), 55; The Mary Evans Picture Library — 10, 15, 53; Exley Publications Picture Library — 34; The Hulton Picture Company — 43; Max and Bea Hunn — 8; The Image Bank — 60; Library of Congress — 33, 37, 38, 40, 44, 50-51, 57; Peter Newark's Western Americana — 7, 14, 16 (lower), 19, 21, 26, 30, 32, 35, 41, 42, 48 (upper), 49, 52; Photo Researchers Inc. — 12, 48 (lower): Gary D. MacMichael — 46 (upper); Stop Pictures: Ron Sandford — 22 (upper); Superstock — cover, 4, 5, 9, 13, 16, 22 (lower), 23, 47; The White House Collection — 11; The White House Historical Association: photograph by the National Geographic Society — 39.

North American edition first published in 1991 by
Gareth Stevens, Inc.
1555 North RiverCenter Drive, Suite 201
Milwaukee, Wisconsin 53212, USA

Library of Congress Cataloging-in-Publication Data

Sproule, Anna.
    Abraham Lincoln / by Anna Sproule.
       p. cm. — (People who have helped the world)
    Includes index.
    Summary: Discusses the life and accomplishments of the sixteenth president of the United States.
    ISBN 0-8368-0216-0
    1. Lincoln, Abraham, 1809-1865—Juvenile literature. 2. Presidents—United States—Biography—Juvenile literature. [1. Lincoln, Abraham, 1809-1865. 2. Presidents.] I. Title. II. Series.
    E457.905.S67   1991
    973.7'092—dc20   [B]   [92]   90-10374

Series conceived and edited by Helen Exley
Picture research: Elizabeth Loving
Editors: Samantha Armstrong and Margaret Montgomery
Series editor, U.S.: Amy Bauman
Editor, U.S.: Barbara Behm
Editorial assistants, U.S.: Scott Enk, Diane Laska, John D. Rateliff, Jennifer Thelen

Printed in Hungary

1 2 3 4 5 6 7 8 9 95 94 93 92 91

ABRAHAM LINCOLN

Leader of a nation in crisis

by Anna Sproule

Gareth Stevens Publishing
MILWAUKEE

The man with the gold pen

At the table by the windows, the tall man reached out and pulled the paper toward himself. With his other hand, he picked up his pen. It was a gold pen, fit for the signature he was about to write. A hush fell over the people who watched him.

As the president of the United States, the man signed papers every day — letters, laws, and countless orders to the army fighting its never-ending war in the South. Many of the papers he signed were pardons for soldiers who had run away from that war, for the man with the gold pen was kindhearted. He knew about sorrow, and he pardoned deserters whenever he could.

But today — this first day of January 1863 — it was more than a pardon that he would be signing. It was a release for a whole people. It was a signal that, for the first time in many generations, they could come fully, legally alive as human beings. When signed, the paper would proclaim the freedom of millions of black slaves, owned and used by the farmers in the South.

"All persons held as slaves"

Leaning forward, the president dipped his pen in the inkwell, drew it out again — and stopped. Frowning, he stared at his hand. It was shaking. This would never do. Carefully, the president set the ink-laden pen down and flexed his fingers. They felt almost numb, and his arm was as heavy as lead.

It was no wonder, given the way he'd spent the morning. Although the country was torn by civil war, it was still New Year's Day. The morning had been the

Opposite: Abraham Lincoln, the sixteenth president of the United States of America, and (below) the Emancipation Proclamation that he signed on January 1, 1863. It gave freedom to almost four million African-Americans, held as slaves in the cotton-growing states of the South.

5

time for the president's New Year party. He had personally greeted each visitor to the White House in Washington, D.C., and had shaken each one's hand.

It was not the best way to prepare for a moment that would make history. The president knew, as well as he knew his own name, that the paper before him would change everything. Thousands of people would see his signature. They'd read it with the same care as they'd read all the other words and lines on the page. He read the paper's most important lines to himself one last time: "I do order and declare that all persons held as slaves within said designated States, and parts of States, are, and henceforward shall be free."

More than freedom

The man knew that these twenty-five words would bring more than freedom. They would also most certainly bring fear and destruction. They had to. That was the idea. The words would wreck the slave owners' prosperity. The words would kill off the whole way of life that the slave owners were fighting to protect. The words would — they must — help bring the whole dreadful war to an end.

And here he was, about to make them law with a wretched, trembling signature. Despite this shaking, however, he had no second thoughts. Nothing was more rock-solid than the president's resolve. Shaking or not, his hand would this day obey his mind and sign his Proclamation of Emancipation.

The president of the United States picked up his gold pen once more. In his sloping, careful handwriting, he wrote his name: Abraham Lincoln.

Towering achievements

Many people consider Abraham Lincoln one of history's great leaders and one of the finest presidents that the United States has ever had. He was an extraordinary man. He was at once humble and ambitious, compassionate and tough, plodding and piercingly intelligent. Even today, more than one hundred years after his death, few leaders have equaled him.

Lincoln is especially remembered for two colossal achievements. He saved his country from self-destruction, and he freed its slaves.

Log cabin birth

The president who freed the slaves was himself born dirt poor. He came into the world on February 12, 1809, in a log cabin beside Nolin Creek in the state of Kentucky. The cabin had a door, a window, a chimney, a mud floor, and not much else. Although it was not much bigger than a shed, it was home to the baby "Abe," his two-year-old sister Sarah, and their parents, Thomas and Nancy Lincoln.

Thomas — a cheerful, sociable character — was a small farmer, who scratched an uncertain living from the Kentucky soil, as had his father before him. Thomas, however, was also a bit of a wanderer, so the Lincolns did not stay long at Nolin Creek. While Abraham was still just a baby, Thomas moved his family a little farther down the stream to Knob Creek. The Lincolns moved again when Abraham was seven, to what was then the newest state in the Union — Indiana.

On the wild frontier

If the family's homes in Kentucky had been remote, the new one in Indiana was on the wild frontier. The Lincolns arrived at Little Pigeon Creek, Indiana, in the dead of winter. Because there could be no house building until the spring came, the family spent the snowy months in a three-sided log shelter. Only a blazing fire on the shelter's open side kept the cold out and the wolves at a distance.

Life for the Lincolns was not easy. In 1818, when Abraham was nine, disaster struck the family. Worn out by frontier life, Nancy Lincoln died. Although she was only in her early thirties, her teeth had fallen out, and her skin had become withered like a dead leaf.

In those days, frontier women, with their skills in home management and medicine, kept their families going. Without Nancy, Thomas could not keep up with his work and look after Sarah, Abe, and Dennis Hanks, a distant cousin who had come to live with the Lincolns. Cabin life soon became chaotic, dirty, and miserable.

After a year of such hardship, Thomas married again. His new wife was a warm-hearted and outgoing widow named Sarah Bush Johnston. With her came her three children: Sarah, John, and Matilde. The Lincoln family had now grown to eight.

As a farmer's son, Abraham Lincoln spent most of his childhood helping his father work the land. He went to school when he could; in all, his formal education totaled little more than a year. But, hungry to know about the world beyond Little Pigeon Creek, Indiana, Lincoln tirelessly read every book he could find. He spent many nights reading by firelight, much as the settler boy in this drawing is doing.

As a boy, Abraham Lincoln wrote this jaunty poem at the bottom of one of his school papers.

Abraham Lincoln
his hand and pen .
he will be good but
god knows When

Sarah — and books

Sarah Lincoln was an especially strong influence on Abraham, who was a somewhat strange child. At times, he fell into deep, brooding silences; at other times, jokes poured out of him. These particular character traits would follow him even into adulthood.

By the time he was ten, Abraham was a hungry reader. He read whatever he could get his hands on: the Bible, *Aesop's Fables*, novels such as *Robinson Crusoe* and *Pilgrim's Progress*; and solid books of facts such as histories and biographies. After reading all these books, Abraham would read them all again — and again. He even read while working in the fields. Sarah encouraged Abraham's desire for knowledge and tried to make certain that he received an education.

Thomas Lincoln did not see much need for reading and writing — certainly not for the boy he was bringing up to be a farmhand. But with Sarah's encouragement and Abraham's own tremendous inner drive, the boy became educated. His formal education, however, was inconsistent. He would attend classes at country schools a month here and a month there, whenever his father could spare him from the fields. In all, Lincoln once estimated, he had spent no more than a year of his life in a classroom.

Thomas Lincoln thought this was quite enough. After all, the things that mattered most in Little Pigeon Creek were births, deaths, harvests, and hard, back-breaking field work. Besides working on the family farm, Abraham was often hired by neighboring farmers — at only twenty-five cents a day. And all of Abraham's earnings automatically went to his father. Only when he turned twenty-one would Abraham be able to keep his own wages and be his own man.

In 1830, Lincoln's twenty-first birthday came and went. That same year, his father grew restless again and moved the family to Illinois. Setting up the new homestead there was just like setting up the old one at Little Pigeon Creek — more snow, more wolves, more trees to fell, and more land to clear.

By this time, Lincoln had had enough of this frontier life. When the snow left in the spring of 1831, Abraham Lincoln went with it. Bidding his family good-bye, he went out into the world to discover a life of his own.

Frontiersmen spent a lot of time cutting down trees to clear land. As a young man, Lincoln — seen here splitting logs to make fence railings — was famous for his skill with an ax. The image of "Abe" as a backwoods railsplitter was seized on by Lincoln's political friends, who used it to boost support for him. Lincoln himself hated memories from his poverty-stricken past.

A man with a difference

Lincoln ended up in Illinois in a brawling riverside settlement called New Salem. There, he landed a job as a clerk at the small country store owned by Denton Offutt. The now more than six-foot-tall Lincoln made friends fast. During working hours, he sent customers at the store into fits of laughter with his uproarious stories. After work, he mixed with some of the other young men at one of the town's saloons. To these men, it must have seemed odd that he did not drink.

But that was not the only thing that did not fit in with the tough frontiersman image that New Salem had of Lincoln. He also joined the local debating society and kept company with some of the educated people in town — the doctor, the schoolmaster, and the innkeeper. At first, the other members of the debating society turned up their noses at their new recruit. They were shocked, however, when the man from "down at the store" turned out to be a first-class natural speaker. Encouraged, Lincoln continued with the self-education that he'd started at Little Pigeon Creek. He studied mathematics and worked hard on English, learning the bare bones of formal grammar. More important, at twenty-three, he went into politics.

Politics and law

When they weren't talking of river transportation or hooting over one of Lincoln's tales, the people in the New Salem store talked politics. What they said always interested Lincoln. To be sure, he'd escaped the backwoods drudgery of his father's farm. But he still wanted to go farther in life than New Salem, Illinois. Young Lincoln wondered if politics would help. It seemed possible; men who went into politics seemed to get ahead fast.

In 1832, Lincoln ran for election to the Illinois state legislature. Although he didn't win, he had impressed the people of his southern Illinois area. Furthermore, the experience left him thirsting for more. Two years later, in 1834, Lincoln tried again. This time, he was elected. When the Illinois legislature came together that winter, it included a lean-faced, rumpled giant of a man, who had his eyes firmly set on the future. By the time his first legislative session had ended, Lincoln had added another ambition to his list. He planned to become a lawyer.

Becoming a lawyer was an extraordinary plan for a frontiersman who still spoke the country dialect of Indiana. But it had also been in Indiana that Lincoln had first fallen under the law's spell. Not long before he left that state, he had discovered the local courtrooms and the legal dramas that took place in them.

Lincoln's first law office was located in Springfield, Illinois: "No. 4 Hoffman's Row, up stairs." There, a room over Tom Dupleaux's furniture store housed little more than a chair, a bench, a bed, and a bookcase for the partnership's law books.

"All men are created equal"

Fascinated, he pored over the United States Constitution — the set of rules by which the United States is governed — and the Declaration of Independence — the statement that the country's founders had written to King George III of Great Britain when the United States broke from British rule in 1776. "We hold these Truths to be self-evident," the Declaration of Independence stated, "that all Men are created equal, that they are endowed by their Creator with certain unalienable Rights, that among these are Life, Liberty, and the Pursuit of Happiness." Lincoln would remember these words all his life.

Inspired by the Constitution and the Declaration of Independence, Lincoln borrowed all the law books he could find and started to study. Three years later, in

1837, the twenty-eight-year-old Lincoln took his legal exams and became a full-fledged lawyer.

Lincoln — in luck . . .

Soon after this, Abraham Lincoln left New Salem to try his luck in Springfield, the town that was to become the state capital. Another young lawyer, John Todd Stuart, asked Lincoln to become his law partner there. Lincoln gladly accepted.

He rode into Springfield on a borrowed horse, with his belongings in saddlebags and his feet dangling to the ground. He had a job and an office to go to but nowhere to live. On top of this, seven dollars was all the money he had in the world. But luck was with Lincoln. Joshua Speed, a storekeeper in Springfield, took a liking to the tall, glum-looking man. He offered Lincoln temporary lodgings over his store — for free. Lincoln settled in, and before long, was making a name for himself as a first-rate lawyer.

. . . and in love

Although Lincoln was miserably shy with women, his social life prospered in culturally minded Springfield. As a professional man, he could visit the city's best families. In 1839, when he was thirty, Lincoln fell in love with one of the smartest, wealthiest women in town: Mary Ann Todd. Todd was originally from Lexington, Kentucky, where her father was a wealthy banker. In Springfield, she lived with her sister Elizabeth and Elizabeth's husband, Ninian Edwards.

Mary Todd Lincoln is seen here in an official White House photograph taken in 1861. The flamboyant daughter of a wealthy Southern banker, she and Abraham Lincoln were married on November 4, 1842.

Like Lincoln, Mary Ann Todd was fascinated by power and politics. But apart from that, she and her tall suitor were very different. She was vivacious and fashionable. She was never shy or at a loss for words. In Kentucky, her family was made up of leading members of Lexington's society. In fact, her family was so rich that they owned slaves.

Abraham Lincoln's family had also come from Kentucky, which was a slave state. Unlike many Kentuckians, however, Thomas Lincoln did not approve of slavery. Far from owning slaves to work for him, he had spent most of his life working his own land. Abraham Lincoln's views on slavery were the same as his father's.

Leaving the past behind

But Abraham Lincoln and Mary Ann Todd had more to contend with than their differences. A greater difficulty to overcome was the fact that the Todd family didn't like Abraham Lincoln or his humble origins. They felt that the lanky lawyer was unsuitable for Mary Ann. But in spite of all their differences and difficulties, Abraham Lincoln and Mary Ann Todd somehow managed to hold on to their love for each other. On November 4, 1842, they were married in the Edwards' grand Springfield home.

The newlyweds' first home was nothing grand. It was a single upstairs room in the Globe Tavern — a Springfield inn. A year later, the couple gave birth to Robert, the first of their four children. Now the room at the inn was growing crowded. Finally, in 1844, with the help of Mary's father, Lincoln and his growing family moved into a beautiful home of their own. It made a good setting for Lincoln's biggest political victory yet. In 1846, the voters of his area chose Lincoln to represent them in the Congress of the United States. Hard times were now behind him forever.

In 1844, Lincoln — by now a prosperous lawyer — bought this Springfield home for his family. Like other people in polite Springfield society, the Lincolns had a maid to do housework, help with the children, and even greet callers at the door. Lincoln, however, often forgot to be formal and would sometimes answer a knock at the door himself.

Lincoln's America

Today, the country known as the United States of America stretches from the Atlantic Ocean in the east to the Pacific Ocean in the west. It is the world's fourth largest country and has a population of about 245 million people.

It wasn't like that in Abraham Lincoln's lifetime. At the start of the 1800s, just before Lincoln was born, the country did not span the continent. Its population was not much greater than five million. The people who, in the 1770s, had rebelled against their British rulers and set up their own nation lived mainly on the country's eastern coast.

Gradually, the country's growing white population expanded westward into the frontier territories. As each territory gained enough people to count as a settled place, it could seek admission as a state. An earlier generation of the Lincoln family had played a full part in this push westward from the family's original base in Virginia. The Lincolns had moved to Kentucky to try their luck on the "dark and bloody ground" that was hotly defended by American Indians already living there. The move brought no good to Abraham's grandfather, also named Abraham, who was killed by Indians there.

The North and the South

Even as colonies, the thirteen states had each had very different characteristics. As the frontier of the United States moved westward, these differences spread, too. But the main dividing line existed between the Northern states and the Southern states. These differences were social, political, and economic.

The South, with its rich soil and warm, damp climate, was primarily agricultural. Before the Civil War, it became a land of huge farms, called plantations. To run these huge tracts of land efficiently, the Southern farmers needed plenty of cheap labor. Thus, slavery became essential to the Southern economy. As slavery took hold, wealthier farmers had time to devote to a more leisurely lifestyle. For a time, this became the Southern ideal.

In contrast, much of the North was still frontier, and life there was often less leisurely. The region generally had smaller farms and the farmers often worked their own land. The North tended to be more industrial, turning its energies to financing the agricultural South or developing manufacturing capabilities for its crops.

Markets, machines — and cotton

From the earliest days of its independence, the United States badly needed goods it could export to Europe in exchange for cash. Very quickly, it found something — cotton. Raw cotton is the white, fluffy lining of the cotton plant's seedpod. The cotton plant grows well in moist, warm climates. The Northern states, of course, were too cold and dry to grow cotton. But in the South, the cotton plant grew like a weed. Across the Atlantic, in Europe, a quickly growing population was eager to buy the cheap, durable fabric that could be made from this "weed."

Europe had the markets. It also had the means to make fabric from the raw cotton with its newly invented machines. Europe, in fact, was going through a huge

The snowy white puffs of a cotton crop cover the land to the horizon. As each puff, or "boll," was picked, it was put into the long, trailing bag tied over the picker's shoulder. Slaves were expected to gather at least 150 pounds (68 kg) of cotton in a day. Here, in a photo taken in 1948, field hands harvest cotton in much the same way as slaves did nearly a century earlier.

13

Cotton was not the only crop grown in the Southern states. The slaves shown here are cutting sugarcane on a plantation in Louisiana. In 1860, when this photograph was taken, there were nearly four million black slaves in the American South — about a third of the South's total population. Among the white Southerners, slave owning on a large scale was a sign of wealth and power. Less than a quarter of the South's whites owned even one slave, and most slave owners had fewer than twenty. But a planter knew he needed a slave work force of at least thirty if he was to become really rich.

upheaval of its own called the Industrial Revolution.

In the United States, the Southern states were quick to spot their opportunity. Early in its history, the South had earned money from growing tobacco and rice. In the mid-1790s, cotton was added to the list and became the crop of choice. The cotton business boomed, and money poured into the South.

The northern United States also profited from this boom. Already the North was turning itself into a wealthy, industrialized area of factories, banks, and businesses. Northern banks lent money to Southern cotton growers. Northern businesses handled the trade between the South and its huge foreign market. Northern factories made both cotton textiles and the machinery to produce them. In short, the South's "cotton kingdom" brought prosperity and growth to everyone in the entire United States — that is, to everyone who was free.

The nightmare of slavery

The founders of the United States had dedicated their country to the idea that all people were created equal. By the time Lincoln entered Congress, however, it had

become a land where some three million people had no rights at all. These people were black slaves — Africans and the descendants of Africans, who had been sold into slavery.

This transatlantic trade in human beings was far older than the "cotton kingdom." It was older than the United States itself. It had been going on since the early 1600s, when the country consisted of just colonies. For over two hundred years, the slave traders had been tearing Africans from their homes and families and plunging them into the nightmare of slavery.

The Africans' torment began as soon as they entered the stinking, suffocating cargo holds of the slave traders' ships for the voyage west. Each adult slave was packed into a space about 30 inches (76 cm) high, 15 inches (38 cm) wide, and less than 79 inches (201 cm) long. Children had much less.

Women and children were usually allowed on deck during the day, but men were not. Once stowed, men had to stay below in their coffinlike spaces. Here they ate, slept, woke, vomited, writhed in fever, went mad, and — if fate was merciful — died. Both men and

Slaves are sold at an auction in Virginia. Flanked by the plump auctioneer, a young black family submits to inspection by the buyers below. The mother and baby will certainly be sold together. But, if the price is right, the auctioneer may sell the father to another owner, splitting the family forever. The white onlookers, meanwhile, treat the auctioneer's hall as a sort of club, dropping in to loiter, chat, and read newspapers.

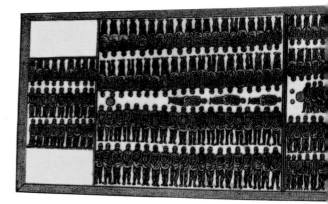

Above: Slaves wait to be sold at a Virginia slave market. To push prices higher, owners always made sure that slaves looked their best before selling them. Thin ones would even be specially fattened up.

women snatched at death if they had the chance by jumping into the sea. But for many, death came to them where they lay, chained down in the putrid darkness. Some lives began there, too. A horrified ship's doctor once reported seeing a slave baby born while its mother was still "shackled to a corpse that [the] drunken overseer had neglected to remove."

Of the millions of Africans that were crammed into the wooden sailing ships, huge numbers did not even survive the journey. A slave-ship captain fully expected to lose an eighth of his human cargo on the voyage to America. Even that was often an underestimate. Ships sometimes arrived in the New World with only two-thirds, half, or even less of their original loads. The rest — the dead and the insane — had gone the way of everything else that the crew regarded as useless: over the side. Sharks followed slave ships all the way across the Atlantic.

A profitable trade

Both American and British slave traders had grown rich on this trade. Then, early in the 1800s, British reformers succeeded in having the slave trade banned from British ships. The United States followed the British example. According to United States law, these victims of "King Cotton" were no longer to be imported. But that made no difference to the slavers. They laughed at the law and gloated over the increased prices that their cargoes would bring. The year Abraham Lincoln entered Congress, healthy slaves were being sold at $2,500 each. The prices were turning slave traders into millionaires.

Without slaves, the cotton crop in the Southern states would not have existed. There would have been no wealth for the Southern planters and no booming foreign trade with the rest of the world. The crop, wealth, and trade were all based on the work that the slaves did — planting the cotton, weeding the cotton,

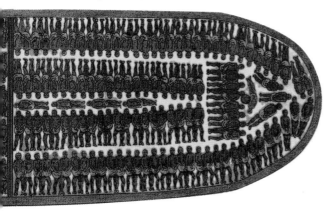

Left: This diagram shows how captured Africans were packed into the hold of a ship for their journey from Africa to the New World. Such a scene was once witnessed by a doctor who, aghast, remembered how the Africans struggled for breath with "all those laborious and anxious efforts for life which are observed in expiring animals, subjected by experiment to foul air." On many ships, slaves were packed even more tightly.

Opposite: Some slaves were freed by their owners. But, for most, there were only two ways out of their slavery: death or escape. To catch runaway slaves, planters in the slave states formed themselves into patrols, as shown here. It took great luck or skill for a slave to elude the patrols, which used both horses and dogs.

and picking the cotton. So, as illegal and blood-tainted as this hideous trade was, it went on.

The life of a slave

The cotton-picking season was a long one, from late summer to the end of the year. Slaves worked from dawn to dusk or longer. They were told when to start work, when to break for food, when to begin again, and when to quit for the night. If they did not do as they were ordered, they were often savagely whipped.

Although they brought great wealth to their owners, the slaves who worked on a cotton plantation saw none of this wealth themselves. They did not, of course, get paid in any way. Many Southerners saw blacks not as people to be employed but as livestock to be used. Owners treated their slaves as well — or as poorly — as other livestock.

Their food, pork and cornmeal, was reasonably good. Without this nutrition, the slaves would not have been able to work efficiently. Their clothing was often flimsy, and shoes were worn only in winter. As for housing, the slave owners' riding horses were often better treated. At least the horses had dry, snug stables, equipped with stalls and mangers. Most slaves had tiny, windowless cabins with dirt floors, and walls through which the wind whistled. Only a few slaves had even the most basic pieces of furniture. Most slept, like cattle, in straw on the floor.

Below: A replica of a Confederate five-hundred-dollar bill.

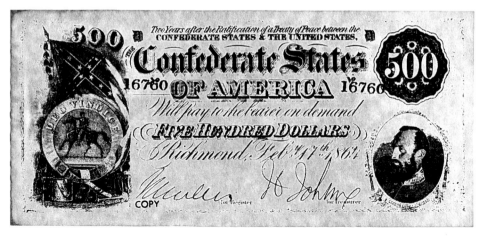

The power of the slave owner

The slave owners did everything they could to make sure their slaves stayed powerless forever. Slaves could not, for instance, buy anything or sell anything. They were not usually allowed to own anything, either. They were not allowed to learn to read and write. They could not get married. They could not give evidence in a court of law. Even to protect themselves, they could never hit a white person.

Above all else, they could not leave their owners' land without permission. Like the land, they were part of their owners' property. If they left, they were robbing their owner. Again, the punishment for this was the whip — at the very least. In theory, of course, owners were not allowed to kill their slaves. But in practice, the law often turned a blind eye. Slaves were whipped, battered, and even burned to death.

As property, slaves could be bought and sold. And sold they were every day in shops and auction rooms all over the South. If a planter was short of money, he simply sold some of his slaves. When a planter died, his heirs sometimes sold the slaves for cash, which made dividing the estate easier. Slaves were even used instead of money by gamblers who would stake a human being against the luck of the cards.

As a result, slave families were often split up. Formal slave marriages were banned, but that did not stop slaves from falling in love or having children. The owners did not mind if slaves had children. Many people saw slave women as breeding machines that could increase their owners' wealth every nine months. Slave women who managed to survive ten childbirths were sometimes given their freedom as a reward. A "good breeder" — as these women were thought of — was then free to come and go.

Her children, however, were not. Nor were all the thousands of ordinary black families, who in conditions close to those of a concentration camp, were trying to lead ordinary family lives. But no matter what they did, and no matter how much they loved each other, they could never escape from the dreadful fear of separation that hung over them. If an owner decided to sell his slaves to different buyers, members of a slave family might never see each other again.

"You say A. is white, and B. is black. It is color then; the lighter, having the right to enslave the darker? Take care. By this rule, you are to be a slave to the first man you meet, with a fairer skin than your own."

Abraham Lincoln, planning his antislavery arguments

"You do not mean color exactly? — You mean the whites are intellectually the superiors of the blacks, and, therefore have the right to enslave them? Take care again. By this rule, you are to be slave to the first man you meet, with an intellect superior to your own."

Abraham Lincoln, planning his antislavery arguments

Rose Williams remembers

What that fear felt like was recalled some years ago by a ninety-year-old black woman named Rose Williams. Williams had once been a slave. As a little girl, she had watched in the crowded auction room as the auctioneer had sold off her father to a planter named Hawkins. After another round of brisk bidding, Hawkins bought little Rose's mother, too. Then it was Rose's turn.

The bidding opened at $400. Quickly it rose to $425 . . . $450 . . . $475. To the child on the auctioneer's block, the men who were deciding her fate were no more than voices — white men's voices coming out of the crowd that milled around her, staring at her.

The price bid for Rose climbed higher and higher. Eventually, the number of voices still bidding dwindled to just two.

"There am tears coming down my cheeks," Williams remembered, "cause I's being sold to some man that would make separation from my Mammy. One man bids $500, and the auction man ask, 'Do I hear more?'" Five hundred dollars! Although it was a fifth of what an adult slave would bring, it was still a lot of money. But the other bidder was prepared to go even higher. At the very last minute, he offered $525.

Bang!

The auctioneer's hammer came down, sealing Rose's fate. She had been sold for $525. And shaking with disbelief and joy, Rose learned that it was the same planter, Hawkins, who had bid $525. She had also been sold to Hawkins. The little family was safe again — for the time being.

A trade like any other? This photograph of a street in Atlanta, Georgia, in the mid-1800s shows a slave dealer's shop sandwiched between two other businesses. For the owner, slave dealing was a business just like any other. By this time, slavery was so embedded in the South's way of life that any threat to it was a threat to the South itself.

Freedom in the North

Although some slaves were eventually freed by their owners, most knew that there could be only two ways out of this horrible life. One was death, and slaves often killed themselves. The other was escape to the North. Although slavery existed in the North, it was less common. And by the time the Civil War erupted, all but four of the states that stayed with the Union had banned this practice.

Although many states in the North did not allow slavery within their borders, Northerners' personal feelings about it were mixed. Many did not question

the Southerners' rights to run their states as they wished. Others, while they supported the idea of freeing the slaves, did not like the idea of blacks living alongside whites.

Of course, some Northerners genuinely opposed slavery, and their numbers were growing. A new feeling of compassion was spreading as people started to react against the harsh realities of the Industrial Revolution. They were discovering how grim life really was for all but the rich. They were demanding reforms. In the North, many of these reformers were abolitionists, and they were committed to abolishing slavery throughout the country. Both Christianity and the Declaration of Independence, they argued, preached the unity of all peoples. Slavery contradicted both and was dividing a country whose very name — the United States — held a strong message of unity.

The South under threat

The Southerners did not take the reformers lightly. They could not afford to because their whole way of life depended on slavery. Without slaves, who would plant the cotton fields? Who would tend these fields and pick the precious harvest? And who would look after the other crops, mend carts and fences, shoe horses, clean houses, cook meals, look after children, make and wash clothes, run messages, and — on top of everything else — show by their very presence just how much money their owners had?

Without the slaves, the life-style and wealth of Southern whites would fall apart. The abolition of slavery was more than a worried view of the future. It was a very real threat, with its source lying in the ever-changing geography of the United States.

Throughout the history of the United States, especially in the decades soon after the Revolutionary War, individual states held much power over their own affairs. There were exceptions to this basic rule, however. If, for instance, three-quarters of the states sought to outlaw slavery by constitutional amendment, the others would have to go along with the decision.

Despite the growing antislavery movement, Southerners felt that as long as the numbers of the slave and free states stayed roughly equal, the South and its

Living conditions in the South ran to extremes. The slave cabin (below) stands in contrast with the slave owner's beautiful home (opposite, bottom). The wealthiest planters — those who owned one hundred or more slaves — had plenty of money to spare to make their mansions splendid. A ballroom like this one in Louisiana (opposite, top) rivaled the elegance of Europe's greatest houses.

way of life were safe. If free states came to outnumber slave states, the South would no longer be safe. As the nineteenth century entered its second quarter, the numbers began changing as more states were added to the Union. Each change took the Union deeper into a conflict that it seemed only war could settle.

The numbers game

In 1820, Congress enacted a series of laws called the Missouri Compromise. These laws, which admitted Missouri as a slave state, also gave the North and South an equal number of twelve states each. From then on, the compromise stated, slavery would not be allowed into any new states that were formed north of Missouri's southern border.

Both sides thought they had done well in this compromise. The South had successfully protected its way of life. The North, meanwhile, was sure that the spread of slavery had been stopped. But the lawmakers had made no allowance for surprises. And in the 1830s and 1840s, surprises started coming fast. The first came in 1836 when Texas, until then a province of Mexico, claimed its independence and asked to be admitted to the United States. Before long, Florida was accepted into the Union as a slave state, and several Northern territories were admitted as free states. The numbers game was running wildly out of control.

California's turn . . .

In 1849, California sought admission to the Union as a free state. Because its territory lay across the old Missouri Compromise line, the question of slavery became a problem again. North and South argued hard and came up with an agreement known as the Compromise of 1850. This new agreement had something in it for both sides. For the North, it included California's admission as a free state. For the South, it included a much stricter law on runaway slaves that forced the North to return escaped slaves to the South.

The abolitionists were naturally appalled by this law and swore to defy it. Supporters of slavery, alarmed by the growing threat to the Southern lifestyle, were not pleased either. Four of the slave states

The price of compassion was high in pre-Civil War America. The owner of the warehouse shown below was a known abolitionist. Since abolishing slavery would have meant the abolition of the Southern way of life, slave owners saw abolitionists as enemies and sometimes retaliated. In this drawing, local slave owners destroy their opponent's livelihood. Some abolitionists lost their lives as well.

even began to think of secession — the ultimate remedy. Before the Union destroyed their way of life, they vowed, they would leave the Union altogether. They thought about it; they talked about it. But that was as far as anyone took this new idea . . . for the moment.

. . . and Kansas and Nebraska

In 1854, a fresh shift in the frontier of the United States provoked yet another crisis. Out of the land acquired in the Louisiana Purchase in 1803, two western territories now emerged — Kansas and Nebraska. Newly settled areas such as these were given the special legal status of "territory" before becoming a state. Would slavery be allowed in these territories or would they be free? The question aroused bitter debate in Congress and throughout the country.

In the end, to the fury of many Northerners, Congress opted for a third choice. The lawmakers' decision, known as the Kansas-Nebraska Act, established the territories but left the question of slavery to be decided by the territories' settlers themselves. This act buried the old Missouri Compromise for good and renewed the possibility of slavery extending westward.

Uncle Tom's Cabin — the book that made a war?

Tension grew unbearable between the two halves of the United States in the early 1850s. In addition to the settlement disputes, a book by Harriet Beecher Stowe shook the Western world to the core. Called *Uncle Tom's Cabin*, the book told of slavery from the slaves' point of view, through slave characters such as Topsy and Little Eva. Depicting the terror, brutality, and despair of slave life, the tale forced people to seriously consider the treatment of slaves.

Millions of copies of the book were sold, and few people were unaffected by its message. In fact, Stowe's book is sometimes listed among the causes of the Civil War, and Lincoln went so far as to call Stowe the "little lady who wrote the book that made this great war." At the very least, the book encouraged the abolitionists. In the free states, the voices calling for the abolition of slavery swelled to a deafening chorus.

"In giving freedom to the slave, we assure freedom to the free — honorable alike in what we give, and what we preserve. . . . The way is plain, peaceful, generous, just — a way which, if followed, the world will forever applaud, and God must forever bless."
Abraham Lincoln, in his annual message to Congress, 1862

"No state, upon its own mere motion, can lawfully get out of the Union."
Abraham Lincoln, in his inaugural address, March 4, 1861

Lincoln and slavery

By the time the Kansas-Nebraska Act had stirred tempers to fresh heights, Lincoln had completed his congressional term and had returned to his law practice in Springfield. To his disappointment, his time in Congress had not been as successful as he had hoped. He was clever, ambitious, and had shown himself to be an able politician and a first-class public speaker. But with his cool reasoning and respect for truth, he had supported unpopular issues and lost much favor. Resignedly, Lincoln settled to work again as a lawyer.

Even though Lincoln was no longer a lawmaker, he took a strong interest in the slavery struggle, and his views on it were shared by many other moderate-minded Northerners. Basically, he hated slavery. More important, he hated the way slavery was dividing his beloved Union, turning it from its ideals of equality and democracy. One day, Lincoln was sure, slavery in the South would die of its own accord, since heavy cotton farming exhausted the soil. If slavery were allowed to spread beyond the cotton areas, however, he felt that its death would never happen.

At the same time, Lincoln was not an abolitionist. He respected the right of the old slave states to run their affairs as they wished — as they were entitled to under United States law. In a free country, Lincoln said, people should even be free to have slaves if that was what the law allowed.

A kind, complex man

Such moderation was one of the main traits of Lincoln's character. This trait was based, not on weakness or ignorance, but on years of hard, self-probing thought. What's more, Lincoln was a kind man, not just with his heart, but with his head. Even as a boy, his stepmother Sarah Lincoln once recalled, Abraham Lincoln had been kind. As a man, the kindness was still in him, but with maturity, it had acquired an extra dimension.

Lincoln's point of view was complicated, based on reason rather than emotion. Lincoln himself knew that it sounded contradictory. He summed up his feelings in a letter he wrote to a friend in 1845, the year Texas entered the Union. "I hold it," he wrote, "to be a paramount duty of us in the free states, due to the Union

The small-town lawyer, Abraham Lincoln, would one day become president of the United States. As his reputation grew, the American public grew hungry for details about him. Lincoln, however, was shy about giving them. He once described himself as "lean in flesh, weighing on an average, one hundred and eighty pounds; dark complexion, with coarse black hair, and grey eyes — no other marks or brands recollected."

of the States, and perhaps to liberty itself (paradox though it may seem) to let the slavery of the other states alone; while, on the other hand, I hold it to be equally clear, that we should never knowingly lend ourselves directly or indirectly, to prevent that slavery from dying a natural death — to find new places for it to live in, when it can no longer exist in the old."

Wanted: leaders for a new party

Although Lincoln didn't know it, his "retirement" from politics would not be for long. In less than ten years, he would be back in Washington again — this time as the most important man in the country. In fact, it was the Kansas-Nebraska affair that changed Lincoln's fortunes. Until then, Northerners who opposed slavery had been split into many political camps. They now realized they had to start pulling together. They did, quickly forming a brand-new political party, known as the Republicans. The party had two main aims: to confine slavery within the boundaries of the old slave states and to keep the troubled Union from falling apart.

The new party needed leaders, but the right people were hard to find. Obviously, these leaders had to be good politicians who had some authority. They also had to be able to speak well and convince a crowd. But more important, they had to be respectable. The typical abolitionist — or so many Northerners thought — was a wild character who would say or do anything to win support. The Republicans wanted someone who breathed good sense and moderation. They wanted someone like . . . Abraham Lincoln.

"A house divided"

In June 1856, the Republican party selected Lincoln as its candidate for the 1858 United States Senate election in Illinois. Although Lincoln, who had officially joined the party just that year, did not win the Senate seat, he quickly made a name for himself within the party. Over the next few years, the Republicans' man in the making would work his way up through the political system again — speaking and debating.

From the start, the party members knew they'd found the right person. Lincoln turned out to be one of

"My . . . object in this struggle is to save the Union, and is not either to save or to destroy slavery. If I could save the Union without freeing any slave I would do it, and if I could save it by freeing all the slaves I would do it; and if I could save it by freeing some and leaving others alone, I would also do that."

Abraham Lincoln, on freeing the slaves

the most dazzling orators in the entire country. During the Senate campaign, Lincoln traveled and spoke throughout Illinois. People turned out by the thousands to hear him debate slavery with his political rival for the Senate, Democrat Stephen A. Douglas. Douglas, an experienced senator who had pushed through the Kansas-Nebraska Act, was a brilliant speaker himself. But he knew he had met his match in Lincoln.

Many thousands more came to know of this brilliant speaker through newspaper accounts of his speeches. The words Lincoln addressed to the 1858 Republican state convention thrilled and stirred the people. In language a child could understand, he first quoted from the Bible: "A house divided against itself cannot stand." Then, switching to his own words, he went on: "I believe this government cannot endure; permanently half slave and half free."

Lincoln then told the convention: "I do not expect the Union to be dissolved. I do not expect the house to fall. But I do expect it will cease to be divided. It will become all one thing, or all the other. Either the opponents of slavery will arrest the further spread of it . . . or its advocates will push it forward, till it shall become alike lawful in all the States, old as well as new — North as well as South."

President Abraham Lincoln

In February 1860, Lincoln went east to speak to a group of New York Republicans. It was the Easterners' turn to be dazzled by the midwestern lawyer with the rumpled hair, high-pitched voice, and deep-set eyes. In New York City's Cooper Institute, a packed audience cheered as Lincoln called for Republicans to stand behind their beliefs.

The South, Lincoln told his listeners, wanted the North to stop calling slavery wrong. "Their thinking it right, and our thinking it wrong, is the precise fact upon which depends the whole controversy. . . . Thinking it wrong, as we do, can we yield to them? Can we cast our votes with their view, and against our own?"

The sophisticated New Yorkers rose to their feet, cheering and clapping, as Lincoln ended: "Let us have faith that right makes might, and in that faith, let us, to the end, dare to do our duty as we understand it."

In May 1860, the Republicans met to decide who they would select to fight for the topmost political job of all — the presidency of the United States. The party nominated Lincoln. Six months later, on November 6, 1860, Abraham Lincoln was elected the sixteenth president of the United States. It was a victory for moderation, for humanity, for reason, and for common sense. And it was a victory that led the United States straight into civil war.

The South breaks away

A Republican had come to the White House. For the slave states of the South, all was lost. All through the 1850s, they'd seen their livelihood and culture come under greater and greater threat. Now, a Republican had been placed in charge of the entire country.

The South saw only one course of action: declare independence and leave the Union while life and livelihood were still intact. It began that simply. On

To the tune of their election campaign song, crowds of Lincoln's supporters parade past his Springfield home. Lincoln, standing by his front door in a white jacket, can be instantly recognized by his height.

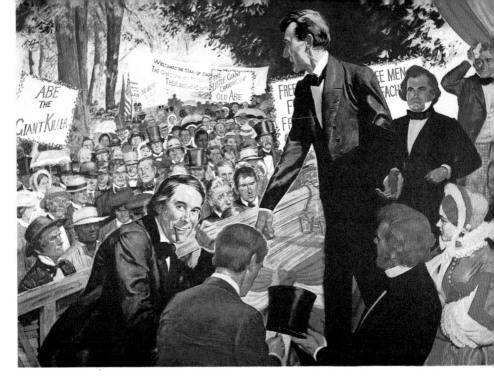

Lincoln debates with his political rival, the famous "Little Giant." Standing no more than five feet (1.5 m) tall, Senator Stephen A. Douglas (second from right) got his nickname both from his size and from his reputation as an orator. His deep, booming voice also added to the impression. Lincoln's voice, in contrast, was high-pitched and shrill. But listeners were struck by the way he could make it carry, even to the back of a large crowd like this one.

December 20, 1860, even before Lincoln had moved to Washington, D.C., the state of South Carolina broke away, or seceded, from the Union. The state declared that it was no longer part of the United States and was thus not bound by the Union's laws. By March 1861, when the new president was sworn in, six other states had also broken from the Union: Alabama, Louisiana, Mississippi, Florida, Georgia, and Texas. With South Carolina, they formed a rival nation, the Confederate States of America, and even elected their own president, Jefferson Davis.

From the lonely heights of his new position, Abraham Lincoln contemplated his own words: "A house divided against itself . . ."

Government by the people, for the people

All his life, Abraham Lincoln had cherished the idea of the United States, with its great union of republics. He cherished the idea of a nation where leaders were chosen not because of their social background or wealth — but because of their abilities and merits. This system made it possible for even ordinary people like himself — a farm boy who had been born in a log cabin and who had known poverty and hunger — to become the country's president.

This was possible in the United States, Lincoln believed, because all things were possible there. A humble background should not bar a person from success. In the United States, hard work, energy, and a good heart were what should matter. True, the South still had a social system where one's background was important, but one day that would fade away along with the farming methods that kept it alive.

Now, however, the whole idea of a union run by ordinary people was falling apart before Lincoln's eyes. Was the idea of government by the people and for the people unworkable? Lincoln would not accept defeat. It *had* to work. The Union had to be saved and the Confederate states had to be brought back into line, by force, if necessary. After all, the way to put down a rebellion was to crush it. If the rebels wanted war, war they could certainly have.

On April 12, 1861, it began. Confederate troops bombarded Fort Sumter, a Union-held army post in Charleston Harbor, South Carolina. After two days, the Union troops surrendered. The American Civil War had begun.

The War Between the States

If the people of the United States had known what they were bringing on themselves that year, even the most headstrong might have thought twice. For the War Between the States, or the Civil War, would be one of the bloodiest, most dreadful conflicts the Western world had yet known. Before it was over, half a million people would die; another half-million would be injured. For a war fought without aircraft and modern weaponry, these are enormous figures.

The Confederate States, or the Confederacy, now consisted of eleven states. The seven original members had been joined by four more: Arkansas, Virginia, North Carolina, and Tennessee. Twenty-three states remained with the Union. These included the free states and, surprisingly, the slave states of Delaware, Maryland, Kentucky, and Missouri. Part of Virginia later broke with the Confederacy to become the separate Union state of West Virginia. Most of the loyal slave

"Let us re-adopt the Declaration of Independence, and with it, the practices, and the policy, which harmonize with it. Let North and South — let all Americans — let all lovers of liberty everywhere — join in the great and good work. If we do this, we shall not only have saved the Union; but we shall have so saved it, as to make, and to keep it, forever worthy of the saving."

Abraham Lincoln, in his speech at Peoria, Illinois, October 1854

*Above: April 12, 1861,
marks the start of the
American Civil War — the
day that the United States
changed forever. The
war's opening shots —
shown here — were fired
by the South. The South-
erners had demanded the
surrender of Union-held
Fort Sumter in Charleston
Harbor, South Carolina.
When their demand was
turned down, they
bombarded the fort
into submission.*

*Opposite: A painting
honors some of the South's
finest military leaders.*

states lay along the border between the two warring
sides. Obviously, keeping them loyal was crucially
important for the Union.

Washington, D.C., which remained the Union's
capital and Lincoln's headquarters, lay at the battlefront.
From his office windows, Lincoln could see across the
Potomac River and right into rebel territory.

The battle begins

Going into the war, the Union seemed to have the
advantages. Its population outnumbered that of the
Confederacy, and its up-to-date industries could provide
its army with the supplies needed to wage a war. But
at first, the South had an asset that the North could not
match — its brilliant generals. The most brilliant of
these was Robert E. Lee, a Virginian of outstanding
abilities and integrity. The Union, with its
inexperienced, sometimes incompetent, generals, was
quickly aware of this weakness. The results of this
mismatch showed on the battlefield.

OUR HEROES
AND OUR
FLAGS

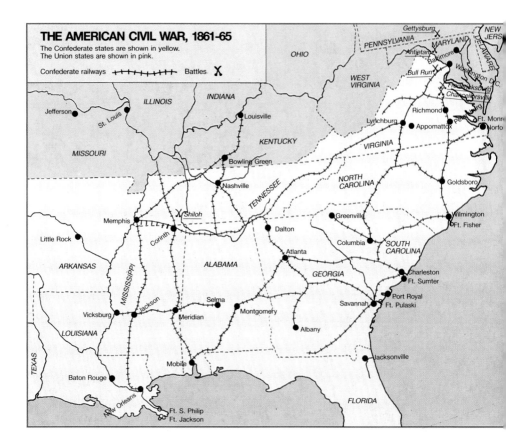

THE AMERICAN CIVIL WAR, 1861-65
The Confederate states are shown in yellow.
The Union states are shown in pink.

Confederate railways +++++++++++ Battles X

OHIO

PENNSYLVANIA
Gettysburg
NEW JERS
MARYLAND
DELAWARE
Antietam
Baltimore
WEST VIRGINIA
Bull Run
Washington D.C.
Fredericksburg
Chancellorsville

Jefferson
ILLINOIS
INDIANA
St. Louis
Louisville
Richmond
Lynchburg
Appomattox
Petersburg
Ft. Monroe
Norfolk

MISSOURI
KENTUCKY
VIRGINIA

Bowling Green
TENNESSEE
NORTH CAROLINA
Goldsboro

Nashville

Memphis
Shiloh
Greenville
Wilmington
Ft. Fisher

Little Rock
Corinth
Dalton
Columbia
SOUTH CAROLINA

ARKANSAS
MISSISSIPPI
ALABAMA
Atlanta
GEORGIA
Charleston
Ft. Sumter

Jackson
Selma
Savannah
Port Royal
Ft. Pulaski

Vicksburg
Meridian
Montgomery

LOUISIANA
Albany

TEXAS
Mobile
Jacksonville

Baton Rouge

New Orleans
Ft. S. Philip
Ft. Jackson
FLORIDA

The United States is seen at the time of the Civil War. The Confederate states, fighting under President Jefferson Davis, are shown in yellow. The Union states, fighting under Lincoln, are shown in pink. West Virginia was originally part of rebel Virginia. But, in 1863, it joined the Union side as a new, separate state.

The first great battle of the war took place on July 21, 1861, along Bull Run Creek near Manassas, Virginia. Known as the First Battle of Bull Run, this clash ended in disaster for the North, which was expecting a quick and easy victory over the rebels. Instead, Confederate troops dug in against the Union advance. Particularly steadfast in his resistance was Confederate general Thomas J. Jackson, whose efforts earned him the nickname "Stonewall." When the Union troops failed to move the Confederate forces, the Union soldiers broke and fled in near panic. Hearing the news, even the soft-spoken Lincoln was enraged.

Bloody Shiloh

The victories of the North were indecisive, and their advances were tiny. Their casualties, however, were huge. In April 1862, for instance, the two sides met in

a two-day battle at Shiloh Church near Pittsburg Landing, Tennessee. In this battle, Confederate general Albert S. Johnston led his troops in a surprise attack on Union troops. Although the Confederate troops finally retreated, it was a bitter victory for the Union troops, here under the command of General Ulysses S. Grant. Union casualties totaled 13,000; the Confederates counted more than 10,000. The Battle of Shiloh proved to be one of the worst of any American war.

All through that summer, Union troops under General George B. McClellan worked their way around eastern Virginia, trying to take the Confederate capital of Richmond. Although they came within easy reach of the city, the Union troops failed. Another 37,000 Union soldiers were lost in the fighting.

In August, the two armies were back at Bull Run. The Second Battle of Bull Run ended in an appalling

Thousands of American soldiers — men from both the North and the South — died at the Battle of Shiloh, which took place near Pittsburg Landing, Tennessee. After this battle, the name Shiloh *became a byword for armed slaughter.*

defeat for the North. Union soldiers made another headlong retreat, leaving behind 14,000 dead, and Confederate troops dug in within twenty miles (32 km) of Washington, D.C.

Abolish slavery?

Although Lincoln was not an abolitionist, many of his supporters were. One day, they were sure, Lincoln would become an abolitionist, too. Soon after the war began, Lincoln's supporters began asking him to abolish slavery in the rebel states — something that no one would have had the power to do in peacetime.

Lincoln listened to them and agreed with their feelings, but he refused their request. He feared that if he abolished slavery, he would lose the support of the all-important border states. These states, although loyal to the Union, were slave states. He could also lose the support of the Democrats, many of whom despised abolitionists and blacks. Despite their differences, people from the various political parties were willing to fight together to save the Union. If Lincoln abolished slavery in the South, this truce between the parties could vanish in a flash. Then the North itself might fall apart, and the South would certainly win.

The abolitionists continued to try to persuade Lincoln. They even added a new argument. Before the war, the South's main cotton customer had been Britain. Some abolitionists feared that Britain might now recognize the Confederacy as an independent country, or even come in on the South's side of the conflict. But the British did not approve of slavery. If the North pledged itself to banning slavery, the abolitionists proposed, the British might not support the South in its fight to preserve the hated institution.

Starting to say "Yes"

Lincoln said "no" to the abolitionists once more. In his heart, though, he had started to say "yes." Personally, he agreed with the abolitionists. How could he not, hating slavery and honoring the Union's ideals of equality and freedom as he did? As a statesman, however, he felt he had to say "no."

But even the statesman in him was beginning to agree with what the abolitionists proposed. After all, his whole aim in the war was to save the Union. If abolishing slavery would do that ... Lincoln examined the idea from all sides. Would banning slavery bring British approval? Yes, it would. Without the slaves, the South could not produce anything. Without products, they could not earn anything. Without money, they could not fund the war. Yes, losing the slaves could certainly damage the South's ability to fight.

But what about the border states? That was the real difficulty. Whatever happened, the border states had to be kept on the Union's side. Resignedly, Lincoln added this to the problems that were crowding him.

Trouble at home

Lincoln's problems were not confined to the presidency. His private life also troubled him at times. Although Abraham and Mary were devoted to each other, they were still very different. He tended to be the quiet one, prone to bouts of gloom and depression. She, all passion and excitement, was occasionally swept away by her fiery temper.

Even before the Emancipation Proclamation was signed, the South's slaves had begun to seize the chances that the war offered them. Once behind the Union lines, refugees like this Virginian family knew they would be safe — and free. Many owners tried to keep slaves from escaping by moving them away from the fighting zones. But, by now, such efforts were useless, as the hold the whites had over blacks was fading fast.

These differences were magnified by the tension-filled time of the Civil War. The fact that Mary Todd Lincoln was a Southerner didn't help matters, either. She had been raised in the Southern life-style, and her brothers were fighting on the Confederate side. Many people in Washington society saw Mary Todd Lincoln as little less than a rebel herself.

But the Lincolns were a strong family. Their children helped keep them that way and were a source of joy, especially to their father. In all, the Lincolns had four sons: Robert, Edward, William ("Willie"), and Thomas ("Tad"). Edward, however, had died in February 1850, more than ten years before the Civil War began. The little boy, barely four years old, died of diphtheria.

Willie and Tad

Thomas ("Tad") Lincoln is shown here with his father. Tad, short for "Tadpole," was a nickname Abraham and Mary Todd Lincoln gave their youngest son at birth.

By the time of the Civil War, then, the Lincolns had only three sons. Robert, the oldest, was almost grown. Willie and Tad, aged eleven and eight, were still bursting with life, high spirits, and mischief. Not even the White House was safe from them — not the bells that Tad set ringing in a fit of wildness; not the strawberries prepared for a state banquet that Tad had eaten well before dinner began; not even the sheets, wrecked by the goat that Tad stabled in his bedroom. Tad, short for "Tadpole," was usually the ringleader, but Willie was nearly as inventive.

The games and laughter went on without stop until both Tad and Willie fell sick with fevers in February 1862. Tad recovered, but Willie did not. His death was a terrible loss to the entire family. It struck Mary Lincoln, who had anguished long over Edward's death, especially hard. Now, left with only her oldest and her youngest sons, she sank deep into depression. For three months, she did not leave her bedroom. The president was stricken to the heart himself. But stubbornly, he went on with the job at hand — trying to save the Union.

Lincoln makes up his mind

Lincoln sketched out tentative plans to abolish slavery. When he presented the plan to the border states,

however, they would have none of it. Lincoln debated with himself again. He realized then that abolition would have to come the hard way — not abolition by consent, but abolition by presidential decree using the powers that the war gave him.

By July 1862, he had made up his mind. He needed to end the war. He needed the slaves to be free people. He needed them to be ready and eager to support the North and maybe even to fight for it. Their freedom lay in his hands, and the time had come for him to give it to them. As commander in chief of the Union army, Lincoln would proclaim the slaves' emancipation.

When Lincoln told his advisers what he was planning, they were stunned. They advised him to wait. They said that his plan was too controversial, too dangerous, and that the timing was wrong. If the North had just won some great victory, things would be different. As things looked now, the president's plan looked like some half-baked attempt to stir up a slave rebellion. Unwillingly, Lincoln agreed that they were right. He would have to wait for a Union victory — if one ever came.

In this painting by Francis B. Carpenter, President and Mrs. Lincoln hold a reception for General Ulysses S. Grant shortly before Lincoln appointed Grant to head the Union armies.

A soldier reads news of the Emancipation Proclamation to a slave family.

What came, on August 31, 1862, was news of the Second Battle of Bull Run. Unfortunately, it had been another terrible defeat for the Union. Days later, on September 5, General Lee and his army invaded slave-owning Maryland, one of the Union's border states. The enemy had now pushed its way into Union territory, moving past the Union capital on its way north.

The Emancipation Proclamation

The Union victory for which Lincoln was waiting did

eventually come. On September 17 that year, Union forces under General McClellan met Confederate forces under General Lee by a stream called Antietam Creek at Sharpsburg, Maryland. After a frenzied battle, the Union won. As usual, the casualties were huge, with over twelve thousand dead on the Union side alone, but it was a victory.

Five days later, on September 22, Lincoln published a preliminary proclamation of emancipation. It promised freedom to all slaves in the Confederate states if the rebels had not made peace with the Union by January 1, 1863. He did not, for a moment, expect that they would.

Nor did they. When the first of January came, the North and South were still locked in combat. With trembling fingers, Lincoln signed the paper that abolished slavery throughout Texas, Arkansas, Mississippi, Alabama, Florida, Georgia, and the Carolinas, and much of Virginia and Louisiana. The exceptions were areas that had already been retaken by the Union or, like West Virginia, had returned to it. The slave-owning border states were exempted, too. The

The news of the North's victory at Antietam Creek gave President Lincoln the confidence he needed to go on with his plan for freeing the slaves. This battle, another of the war's bloodiest, claimed a total of nearly twenty-one thousand casualties from the two sides.

proclamation did not affect slavery in those areas. It was now more vital than ever that those states remained loyal to the Union. There would be time to do something about them later — if the North won.

Lincoln's great decision could have lost him the war. It didn't. But it did lose him a huge amount of popular support. In October 1862, not long after the preliminary emancipation proclamation was signed, another round of elections had taken place in the North. In state after state, the Republicans were ousted by their Democratic rivals.

The people who opposed abolition, feared blacks, and especially feared that freed black slaves would come flooding north to settle and work among whites, now gave their support to the Democrats. They had joined in the war effort, they declared, to save the Union, not to end slavery. Very soon, their protests turned into a full-fledged "stop the war" campaign. Lincoln now fought a war on two fronts, both in the South and at home in the North.

The painting opposite shows the Union army attacking that of the Confederates at Vicksburg, Mississippi. This painting captures the heroic image that many people from both the North and the South held of the war. In the photograph below, a wounded soldier is tended by a comrade. The photograph more accurately captures the war's real-life battlefield conditions.

At first, the Union army was made up of volunteers. But in 1863, the North began calling up all fit men between the ages of twenty and forty-five. Northerners were enraged, and antidraft riots broke out in several cities. During the riot captured in this drawing, rioters set fire to the New York draft office. They then turned their murderous fury on the city's black people. By the time the New York riot was brought under control, five hundred people had died.

The darkest hour

On the battlefield, the Union was dealt blow after terrible blow. In December 1862, Union forces, led by General Ambrose E. Burnside, attempted to cross the Rappahannock River near Fredericksburg, Virginia. Because of delays, however, by the time the 130,000-strong Union army had crossed the river, Confederate forces were firmly entrenched on the other side.

The resulting battle on December 13, known as the Battle of Fredericksburg, cost the Union over twelve thousand soldiers. A month later, in January 1863, Burnside tried to cross the same river again. This advance proved to be nothing more than a "mud march," as the Union army became bogged down in the mud brought on by the winter rains.

May of 1863 saw the Battle of Chancellorsville unfold in Chancellorsville, Virginia. Union troops, still close to the Rappahannock River, fought yet another battle. This time, the Union lost another seventeen thousand men. Hardened as he was to disaster, even Lincoln paled as he heard the news of this latest defeat. It was the Union's darkest hour.

But by the end of the month, good news began coming in from General Grant. Like a sharp-toothed bulldog, Grant had been steadily working his way south along the Mississippi River for months. At last, he was beginning to have some success.

In the northeast, however, things continued to look bleak. In June, General Lee pushed into Union territory again, marching through Maryland and on into Pennsylvania. At any moment, Northerners feared, Confederate troops could swing east and attack Washington, D.C., itself. The attack never came.

Gettysburg

But on July 1, 1863, the armies of the North and South did collide in Gettysburg, Pennsylvania. The little town became the battleground for the bloodiest battle the war had yet seen. By its end, two days later, over forty thousand men lay dead or wounded, but the Union had won. The rebels retreated south.

Then on July 7, news came from General Grant that sealed the North's victory. Vicksburg, Mississippi, a city on the Mississippi River that his troops had been attacking since May, surrendered. The tide was turning in favor of the North.

Today, the name of Gettysburg is as well known as those of Trafalgar, Waterloo, or many other places known for battles that took place at them. But Gettysburg's fame comes not just from the battle that took place there; it is also known for what happened there afterward.

On November 19, 1863, 150,000 people gathered on a hill outside Gettysburg. There, the crowd watched as President Abraham Lincoln dedicated a national cemetery on the very site of the Battle of Gettysburg. Standing in the bright sunshine that day, the people listened for two hours to statesman Edward Everett, who was serving as the ceremony's main speaker. Then it was President Lincoln's turn to speak.

Lincoln's speech did not last two hours. In fact, it lasted just a little over two minutes. Some of the listeners were startled by this short, simple dedication. Most, however, responded with warm applause to the speech that has since become Lincoln's famous Gettysburg Address. The moving words that Lincoln spoke that day stand as a milestone in the history of democracy itself.

"This is essentially a people's contest. On the side of the Union, it is a struggle for maintaining in the world, that form, and substance of government, whose leading object is, to elevate the condition of men — to lift artificial weights from all shoulders — to clear the paths of laudable pursuit for all — to afford all, an unfettered start, and a fair chance, in the race of life."
Abraham Lincoln, in his Independence Day message to Congress, 1861

45

Honoring the more than 650,000 citizens who lost their lives in the Civil War continues even today. Above is the Vicksburg National Cemetery, as it stands today. At right, a photo captures a train on its way to Gettysburg on the day before the cemetery's dedication ceremony. Lincoln is probably the figure in the tall hat, next to the train. Although no one knew it, he was ill at the time with a type of smallpox.

The Gettysburg Address

Fourscore and seven years ago our fathers brought forth on this continent a new nation, conceived in liberty and dedicated to the proposition that all men are created equal.

Now we are engaged in a great civil war, testing whether that nation or any nation so conceived and so dedicated can long endure. We are met on a great battlefield of that war. We have come to dedicate a portion of that field as a final resting-place for those who here gave their lives that that nation might live. It is altogether fitting and proper that we should do this.

But, in a larger sense, we can not dedicate — we can not consecrate — we can not hallow — this ground. The brave men, living and dead, who struggled here, have consecrated it, far above our poor power to add or detract. The world will little note, nor long remember, what we say here, but it can never forget what they did here. It is for us the living, rather, to be dedicated here to the unfinished work which they who fought here have thus far so nobly advanced. It is rather for us to be here dedicated to the great task remaining before us — that from these honored dead we take increased devotion to that cause for which they gave the last full measure of devotion — that we here highly resolve that these dead shall not have died in vain — that this nation, under God, shall have a new birth of freedom — and that government of the people, by the people, for the people, shall not perish from the earth.

"We are met on a great battlefield," Lincoln said at opening ceremonies for the national cemetery in Gettysburg, Pennsylvania. The day — November 19, 1863 — was windy, and the president had difficulty making his voice carry to the crowd's edge. Afterward, he was depressed by what he thought was the crowd's lukewarm reception to his speech. Little did he know that it was to become one of the most celebrated speeches in U.S. history.

Ulysses S. Grant

General Ulysses S. Grant had attracted President Lincoln's notice early in the war. Grant was an extraordinary figure. Unlike the other Northern generals, he fought like a demon. Shiloh, with its bloodstained outcome, had been his work. Later, while stationed in the Mississippi Valley, he had concentrated on attacking the Confederates on their long southern flank. Through his efforts, the Union had taken Vicksburg and had cut the Confederacy in half.

After this victory, Lincoln felt certain that Grant was the man he had been looking for to command the Union forces. So, in March 1864, Lincoln named Grant as the general in chief of all the Union armies. Grant at once took over the war in the East, leaving command of the West to one of his generals, William Tecumseh Sherman. Sherman was a man as tough and resourceful as his commander.

All through the summer, the two commanders kept pressure on the Confederacy — attacking, losing, attacking, digging in, attacking again. . . . The Union's losses were terrible, but it kept sending in more men.

And soon the Union had a new source of volunteers: slaves. As Union lines moved south, thousands of black slaves found refuge and freedom behind those lines. Many of the former slaves enlisted in the Union army. Free blacks from the North enlisted, too. By the war's end, almost 200,000 blacks had joined the Union army, fighting for their own freedom. Lincoln had been right to think he might need them. They were now playing a major part in fighting the war.

Should he give in?

For a while, though, it looked as if the Union might still lose the war. In spite of Gettysburg, in spite of everything Grant and Sherman did, the Confederates remained unbeaten. Worse yet, the war had become unpopular in the North. The people longed for peace. Lincoln had lost much favor with them. Whether or not he lost the war, it certainly looked as if he would lose the upcoming presidential election.

The shifting moods in the North made Lincoln's determination waver. Should he give in, tear up his freedom plan, and make peace with the South? For one dreadful minute, on August 24, 1864, he began to seriously consider giving in. But the idea of allowing slavery to continue appalled Lincoln now. With that in mind, he was again determined to stay with his freedom plan. As for the election, Lincoln decided he would have to risk it.

The end of the tunnel?

In September, the North's luck turned once and for all. On September 2, 1864, Sherman captured one of the greatest cities of the "cotton kingdom" — Atlanta, Georgia. From there, later in the year, he would begin a 250-mile (402-km) march to the East Coast. William T. Sherman would forever after be known for this "March to the Sea," which sliced through enemy country like a sword, destroying everything in its path. His code was total war, waged against both military and civilian populations. By Christmas that year, a great path of devastation marked his march.

The news of Sherman's triumph in Atlanta had an electrifying effect on the North. The Union army

Opposite: Free African-Americans fought to defend freedom. Escaped slave Harriet Tubman (top) helped three hundred other runaways reach the North and liberty via a secret escape system known as the Underground Railroad. American abolitionists created the system. During the Civil War, Tubman worked as an intelligence agent for the Union.

Below: Many Confederates refused to treat black Union soldiers as prisoners of war. When Confederate troops captured this fort in 1864, their black prisoners were burned alive or shot.

By 1865, devastation like this could be seen throughout the South. Much of it was the work of General William T. Sherman on his infamous "March to the Sea." But the destruction of Richmond, Virginia (shown here), was the work of Confederate troops. Rather than let their capital city fall intact to Union troops, Confederates set fire to it.

redoubled its efforts as spirits lifted. In November, the upturn of events brought Lincoln more good news. With ease, he won a crushing victory over his Democratic rival, General George B. McClellan, in the presidential election.

Finally, five months later, on Sunday, April 9, 1865, Confederate general Robert E. Lee met Union general Ulysses S. Grant at Appomattox Court House in Virginia. Outflanked and outfought, the great Southerner surrendered to his opponent there, where so much of the fighting had taken place.

The United States of America was united once more. Delirious with joy, Washington, D.C., and the

entire North celebrated the victory. Bands played, bells rang, and people crowded the streets cheering the Union and the president.

Inside the White House, however, Abraham Lincoln was working harder than ever. The North had won the war. Now, somehow, it had to win the peace. In addition, the war-ravaged country had to be repaired. Finally, the one-time rebels had to be persuaded to accept a completely new way of life — one without slaves. The task looked daunting, but Lincoln was determined. What was more, he was determined to win the peace *peaceably* with, as he said, "malice toward none; with charity for all."

"I know what hole he [General William T. Sherman] went in at, but I can't tell what hole he will come out of."
Abraham Lincoln, speaking
of General Sherman
during Sherman's
"March to the Sea"

When the shot came

April 14, 1865, was Good Friday, the Friday before Easter. But for Lincoln, his mind now consumed with the country's reconstruction, it was business as usual: meetings, decisions, signatures. For history, however, it was to become a day of infamy.

That evening, Abraham and Mary Todd Lincoln attended a performance of the play *Our American Cousin* at Ford's Theatre in Washington, D.C. They arrived after the play had already started, but the entire audience rose to its feet in applause when they entered. Outside the president's box, Lincoln's bodyguard for the evening stood watch for a while. Then, unbelievably, the guard left his post.

In the middle of the third act, a shot rang out. For a second, the world stood still. No one moved, spoke, or breathed. Then, as shrieks erupted from the president's box, a man with a knife stabbed another member of the Lincoln party. Jumping from the box, the assailant landed with a crash on the stage below, breaking his leg. He staggered wildly for a moment, then vanished from sight behind the scenery and escaped from the theater.

All eyes went back to the box, where three people bent over a fourth. The president of the United States slumped motionless in his chair. Unconscious from the assassin's bullet, Abraham Lincoln lay dying. As an army doctor struggled to Lincoln's side, the audience erupted in panic. The president, accompanied by his wife, was carried to a house across the road, and there he was placed on a bed.

In the confusion, Lincoln's attacker escaped, but not before many people had recognized him. The assassin was an actor named John Wilkes Booth, who, it was known, was deeply devoted to the South. Because of this devotion, Booth saw Lincoln as the South's destroyer. In the theater, he had been heard to yell, in Latin, "Thus always to tyrants!" Swiftly, armed search parties were sent out to hunt Booth down.

Lincoln's vice president, Andrew Johnson, was summoned to the scene. An anguished crowd surrounded the house where the president lay, waiting for news. It was morning before news came. At 7:22 A.M. on Saturday, April 15, 1865, Abraham Lincoln

Abraham Lincoln is shot in Ford's Theatre on April 14, 1865. Clutching a dagger in his free hand, John Wilkes Booth enters the presidential box and shoots Lincoln in the back of the head. Although Booth escaped, he was tracked down and killed within days.

"A character so externally uncouth, so pathetically simple, so unfathomably penetrating, so irresolute and yet so irresistible, so bizarre, grotesque, droll, wise and perfectly beneficient."
From Abraham Lincoln's obituary in the New York Herald

"Never had the nation mourned so over a fallen leader. Not only Lincoln's friends, but his legion of critics — those who'd denounced him in life, castigated him as a dictator, ridiculed him as a baboon, damned him as stupid and incompetent — now lamented his death and grieved for their country."
Stephen B. Oates, in his book With Malice Toward None: The Life of Abraham Lincoln

died. He was the first — but not the last — president of the United States to be assassinated.

Lincoln's plans

By the end of the Civil War, the Emancipation Proclamation of 1863 and the Union armies had brought freedom to 3.5 million slaves. But by the time Abraham Lincoln died, he had already taken his emancipation plan a big step farther. He knew quite well that when peace came, his wartime proclamation could be overturned. Furthermore, it freed only the black people in the rebel states and left the rest still enslaved. Therefore, soon after his reelection, Lincoln had asked Congress to approve a sweeping new law. This law, an amendment to the Constitution itself, would ban slavery everywhere within the United States.

In January 1865, Congress agreed to Lincoln's proposal. By a slim margin, the Constitution gained its Thirteenth Amendment by the end of that year. It declared: "Neither slavery nor involuntary servitude, except as a punishment for crime whereof the party shall have been duly convicted, shall exist within the United States." When it became law, it freed all the slaves everywhere in the United States.

That was not the end of Lincoln's plans. Shortly before the Civil War, the United States Supreme Court had decided that even free blacks were not and could not be citizens of the United States. After the war, Lincoln's goal was to bring black Americans into full membership in American society — its public life, its schools, and all the other chances it offered whites to progress and prosper.

One important key to this membership was the right to vote. Before the war, only three Northern states had allowed blacks to vote in their elections. Now, after four years of bloodshed, it was painfully obvious that the former slave owners of the South would not think of such a proposal. Many people in Lincoln's own party also hated it, but the party radicals constantly urged Lincoln to press ahead with giving blacks the right to vote.

Caught between these conflicting interests, Lincoln was still struggling to find solutions to the issue when he was killed.

The Reconstruction Amendments

After Lincoln's death, however, Congress made blacks' rights — freedom, citizenship, and the vote — conditions for letting the rebel states back into the Union. The Thirteenth, Fourteenth, and Fifteenth Amendments, which spelled out these rights, became known as the Reconstruction Amendments.

The Fourteenth Amendment declared that "all persons born or naturalized in the United States, and subject to the jurisdiction thereof, are citizens of the United States and of the State wherein they reside." It became law in 1868.

The Fifteenth Amendment stated that "the right of citizens of the United States to vote shall not be denied or abridged by the United States or by any State on account of race, color, or previous condition of servitude." It became law in 1870.

The South fights back

By 1870, then, U.S. law had abolished slavery throughout the country and guaranteed black people in

On April 21, 1865, Americans from all across the nation came onto the streets to pay homage to their dead president. A train carried Lincoln's coffin from Washington, D.C., to Springfield, Illinois, where it was buried. Here, watched by throngs of mourners, the coffin nears its destination.

Opposite: By the late
1860s, African-Americans
were in theory equal to
whites. But in both the
North and the South, many
white Americans violently
opposed black equality. As
shown in this cartoon,
white opposition fell into
three powerful groups: the
Northern industrialists
(right), the Southern
landowners (middle, with
whip in pocket), and the
Northern industrial work
force (left). Beneath their
boots, a black war veteran
struggles to rise to his feet.

the country equal rights with white people. That, at least, *was* the law. Despite the law, most white Southerners refused to accept the idea that black people were their equals. The whites soon realized they could frustrate the spirit of these laws with laws of their own.

Whites had been doing this since the Civil War had ended and killed off the South's old slave code. In fact, the war was scarcely over before the Southern states started making new rules to keep the newly freed blacks oppressed. These rules, called "black codes," were based on the old slave codes. According to the codes, for instance, the one-time slaves still had to call their employers "master" or "mistress," just as they did before the war. In South Carolina, blacks were allowed to take only jobs such as those they had done as slaves: field hands, nursemaids, cooks. In Mississippi, blacks were forced to travel in separate train carriages from those in which whites traveled. In Florida, the rules made sure that blacks worshiped in separate churches. A black person who tried to join white people in prayer was punished in the traditional Southern way — with the whip. These are just a few examples of how the codes affected the lives of black people.

The Fourteenth and Fifteenth Amendments to the Constitution were designed to do away with these codes. But persistent whites resurrected the old ways yet again with laws known as Jim Crow laws. These laws, named for a popular minstrel show character, were designed to keep blacks "separate but equal" to whites. The laws affected many parts of society. Blacks had separate, often inferior, facilities for everything from schools to public bathrooms. Jim Crow laws came into being in the late 1800s, taking away much of what had been gained in the post-Civil War period called Reconstruction.

Blacks lose ground

If black people dared to exercise their legal rights, they risked a visit from hooded members of the Ku Klux Klan. This secret terrorist society formed shortly after the Civil War as a means for whites to remain in power. Klansmen used threats, beatings, and murder to terrorize and control blacks and sometimes their supporters. A black victim who escaped with a tarring and feathering

*"No man is good
enough to govern another
man, without that
other's consent."*
Abraham Lincoln, in his
speech at Peoria, Illinois,
October 1854

got off lightly, brutal though this treatment was. Often, blacks were lynched, or illegally hanged. Between the 1880s and 1919, Klansmen lynched some three thousand blacks who had dared to insist on equality.

Southern blacks watched as all the gains Lincoln and the war had brought them were whittled away. The right to vote, the right to earn, the right to be a self-respecting member of the national community — what good were these, in a society determined to keep blacks separate, terrified, and poor? In despair, many blacks headed north, but found things were little better there. Trade unions did not like admitting them. They were forced into the lowest-paid jobs. They had to live in the shabbiest, poorest areas of towns. Worse yet, the Ku Klux Klan followed them north.

As grim as things still looked, changes were on the way. The one-time slaves and their children had begun to fight back. By this time, Abraham Lincoln — the one man who might have brought black and white Americans together in the 1860s — was long dead. His role as a hero and a champion of black people was now being filled by blacks themselves. Powerful black organizations were emerging. The National Association for the Advancement of Colored People (NAACP) pledged itself to achieve true freedom for black people in the United States. Black leaders were emerging, too. As the century went on, their stature and power grew.

"I have a dream"

On August 28, 1963, a century after Lincoln's proclamation, a quarter of a million Americans marched on Washington, D.C. It was the biggest single demonstration in the history of the civil rights movement. The group, led by civil rights leader Martin Luther King, Jr., came to celebrate the centennial of the emancipation. In Washington, the marchers gathered around the Lincoln Memorial — the memorial built to honor the man who had made the abolition of slavery a reality. The posters that the marchers carried testified to the way Lincoln's wishes had been carried out. "We seek the freedom in 1963 promised in 1863," stated one. Another stated, "A century-old debt to pay."

This was the day that King would make the speech of his life. This speech, like the Gettysburg Address,

"Go home to Africa."
Antiblack poster in
Alabama, 1950s

"The underclass in America is predominantly black."
From the Times (London),
on racial tension in
New York, 1990

now stands as a landmark in history. "I . . . have a dream, . . ." King began that day. "I have a dream that one day this nation will rise up and live out the true meaning of its creed: 'We hold these truths to be self-evident: that all men are created equal.'

"I have a dream that one day on the red hills of Georgia, the sons of former slaves and the sons of former slave owners will be able to sit down together at the table of brotherhood.

"I have a dream that one day, even the state of Mississippi . . . will be transformed into an oasis of freedom and justice.

"I have a dream that my four little children will one day live in a nation where they will not be judged by the color of their skin but by the content of their character."

In 1968, King himself would be dead, another victim of an assassin's bullet. But even then, less than five years later, King's dream — which was Lincoln's dream — was moving closer to fulfillment. This movement continues today as more and more blacks are crossing the barriers that once kept them from good jobs, homes, and lives. There is still a long way to go, however. In general, blacks in the United States remain poorer than whites. And when an international summit meeting was held in Houston, Texas, in 1990, the Ku Klux Klan still paraded its views and its sinister garb. Over the heads of the marching Klansmen flew the "Stars and Bars," the Confederate flag that once led the South into the Civil War.

So even today, in many ways, the War Between the States is still not over. When it is over, Lincoln's dream can finally, really take hold, and the tasks he began over a century ago can be completed. Then, as Lincoln dreamed, the United States will be a nation truly living by its own creed.

For More Information . . .

Organizations

The following organizations can provide information about Abraham Lincoln's life and career, about the Civil War, or about civil rights and problems minorities still face today. Write to them if you would like to know more about topics of interest to you. When you write, be specific about what you want to know and always include your name, age, and return address.

Abraham Lincoln Museum
Lincoln Memorial University
Harrogate, TN 37752

Civil War Society
P.O. Box 770
Berryville, VA 22611

American Civil Liberties Union (ACLU)
132 West 43rd Street
New York, NY 10036

Congress of Racial Equality (CORE)
1457 Flatbush Avenue
Brooklyn, NY 11210

Civil War Round Table Association
P.O. Box 7388
Little Rock, AR 72217

Lincoln Institute for Research
and Education
1001 Connecticut Avenue NW, Suite 1135
Washington, DC 20036

Confederate Memorial Association
Confederate Memorial Hall
1322 Vermont Avenue NW
Washington, DC 20005

National Association for the Advancement
of Colored People (NAACP)
4805 Mt. Hope Drive
Baltimore, MD 21215

Books

About Abraham Lincoln —

Abe Lincoln: Log Cabin to White House. Sterling North (Random House)
Abe Lincoln: The Young Years. Keith Brandt (Troll)
Abe Lincoln Grows Up. Carl Sandburg (Harcourt Brace Jovanovich)
Abraham Lincoln. Rae Bains (Troll)
Abraham Lincoln. David R. Collins (Mott Media)
Abraham Lincoln. Gabriella Cremaschi (Silver, Burdett and Ginn, Inc.)
Abraham Lincoln. Ingri D'Aulaire and Edgar P. Parin (Doubleday)
Abraham Lincoln. Larry Metzger (Franklin Watts)
Abraham Lincoln. Katie B. Smith (Julian Messner)
Abraham Lincoln: Sixteenth President of the United States. Jim Hargrove
    (Childrens Press)
Lincoln. Andrew Lee (David & Charles)
The Lincoln Country — In Pictures. Russell Freedman (Clarion/Ticknor & Fields)
Mr. Lincoln's Inaugural Journey. Mary K. Phelan (Crowell Junior Books)
The Story of Ford's Theatre and the Death of Lincoln. Zachary Kent (Childrens Press)
The Story of the Gettysburg Address. Kenneth Richards (Childrens Press)

About the Civil War and Slavery —

Anthony Burns: The Defeat and Triumph of a Fugitive Slave.
Virginia Hamilton (Knopf)
Behind Rebel Lines: The Incredible Story of Emma Edmonds, Civil War Spy.
Seymour Reit (Harcourt Brace Jovanovich)
Captive Bodies, Free Spirits: The Story of Southern Slavery.
William J. Evitts (Julian Messner)
Civil War. (Wonder-Treasure Books)
Go Free or Die: A Story about Harriet Tubman. Jeri Ferris (Lerner)
The Red Badge of Courage. Stephen Crane (Airmont)
Rifles for Watie. Harold Keith (Harper & Row Junior Books)
The Story of the Battle of Bull Run. Zachary Kent (Childrens Press)
Uncle Tom's Cabin. Harriet Beecher Stowe (Airmont)

Glossary

abolitionists
The people who opposed slavery for moral reasons and who worked to have it done away with, or abolished. The abolitionist movement began in Europe in the late eighteenth century and spread to the United States, where, initially, the abolitionists were unpopular in both the North and South. By the mid-1800s, however, their numbers had grown enough to make slavery a central issue in American politics, thus making that issue a contributing cause of the Civil War.

border states
Those states — Missouri, Kentucky, Maryland, and Delaware — that lay between the South and the North. Although proslavery, these states remained loyal to the Union during the Civil War. Many people from these states supported the Southern cause, and some of them even fought for the Confederacy.

Compromise of 1850
A series of acts designed to resolve tensions between the North and South. The compromise granted California statehood as a free state, organized the rest of the land gained from Mexico in the Mexican-American War into territories that could choose for themselves whether to be slave or free, settled disputes over the Texas boundary claims, prohibited the slave trade in the District of Columbia, and toughened fugitive slave laws.

dialect
A variety of a language used by a particular group or in a particular area.

Emancipation Proclamation
A statement issued by President Abraham Lincoln freeing, or emancipating, the slaves in the Confederate states. The document, which took effect on January 1, 1863, was designed to win foreign approval for the Union cause. It excluded all

61

slaves in the border states (Missouri, Kentucky, Maryland, and Delaware) as well as those in Union-occupied parts of the Confederacy.

Fort Sumter
A U.S. military fort in Charleston, South Carolina. When South Carolina declared its independence, it asked the United States to turn over the fort to local control. After months during which the Southerners negotiated for peaceful transfer with first President James Buchanan and then President Abraham Lincoln, the Confederates attacked when they learned that Lincoln was sending reinforcements. Fort Sumter quickly surrendered. This first skirmish of the Civil War ended with only one casualty, when a man was accidentally killed during the flag-lowering ceremony.

Industrial Revolution
The historical period marked by a changeover from muscle power to machine power that revolutionized Western production methods in the late eighteenth and early nineteenth centuries. Starting in Europe, the Industrial Revolution spread to the United States in the 1780s.

Kansas-Nebraska Act
The act that divided a single section of land lying west of Missouri into the territories of Kansas and Nebraska. This act sought to resolve the quarrel over whether the Kansas-Nebraska territory should be free or slave by dividing the disputed area into two territories and allowing the settlers in each section to decide for themselves.

Lincoln-Douglas Debates
A famous series of seven debates in 1858 between U.S. senator Stephen A. Douglas, of Illinois, and Illinois lawyer Abraham Lincoln, his Republican challenger. Although Lincoln lost the election, the speeches he gave and the serious challenge he had given to one of the Democratic party's leading spokesmen made him nationally famous.

Missouri Compromise
An agreement set by Congress in 1820 designed to limit the spread of slavery. This action came about when Missouri, a slave-holding territory, applied for statehood. To settle the debate that this application aroused, Speaker of the House Henry Clay proposed a compromise that called for admitting Missouri and Maine (which was also applying for statehood) as slave and free states respectively, thereby maintaining the balance of free and slave states. The compromise also included a law stating that no new slave state could be created north of Missouri's southern border.

North
The part of the United States that gradually excluded slavery and which supported the Union cause in the Civil War. The North contained most of the shipping and manufacturing companies in the United States, and greatly outnumbered the South in terms of population.

paradox
A statement that seems contradictory but could possibly be true.

Reconstruction
   The period following the Civil War during which the United States reorganized and rebuilt itself while restoring the rebel states to the Union.

secession
   The act of seceding, or withdrawing, from something. The Southern states maintained that since they had joined the United States of their own free will, they could leave it in the same way. The first state to do so, South Carolina, repealed its ratification of the Constitution in December 1860. The Northern states, however, held that once a state had joined the United States, it became an integral part of the whole country and lost the right to act independently.

slave trade
   The transportation and selling of humans as slaves. The modern slave trade developed alongside the discovery and colonization of the New World. North American colonists began importing slaves from Africa in 1619. The slave trade was abolished in the United States in 1808, but even after that, slaves could still be sold by people in one state to people in another.

slavery
   The social system in which one person claims to own another. Slaves are the property of their masters. They receive no pay for their work, have no control over their working conditions, and can also be bought or sold. In the United States, slavery was abolished by the Thirteenth Amendment in 1865, and former slaves were made citizens by the Fourteenth Amendment.

South
   Those states which supported slavery and the Confederate cause. Although it included only about a third of the country, the South produced most of America's presidents and military leaders, as well as most of its foreign trade.

unalienable
   Not able to be taken away or given up.

Uncle Tom's Cabin
   A novel written by Harriet Beecher Stowe and published in 1852. This immensely popular tale portrayed the misfortunes and sufferings of a kindly black slave. By describing all the horrors that could go along with slavery, the book created wide public support for the abolitionists and stirred up anti-Southern feelings throughout the North.

Chronology

1808   The United States outlaws the slave trade.

1809   February 12 — Abraham Lincoln is born in a log cabin beside Nolin Creek, Kentucky. He is the second of Thomas and Nancy Lincoln's three children.

1811	Thomas Lincoln moves his family to Knob Creek, Kentucky.
1816	The Lincolns move to Little Pigeon Creek, Indiana. Indiana becomes the nineteenth state to enter the Union.
1818	Nancy Lincoln, Abraham's mother, dies at about age thirty-four.
1819	Thomas Lincoln, Abraham's father, marries Sarah Bush Johnston.
1820	The Missouri Compromise is enacted. Part of the compromise prohibits the creation of new slave states anywhere north of Missouri's southern border, thus limiting the spread of slavery.
1828	Lincoln takes a flatboat trip down the Mississippi River to New Orleans.
1830	Thomas Lincoln moves his family to Illinois. Abraham Lincoln takes a second flatboat trip to New Orleans.
1831	At twenty-two, Lincoln leaves home and moves to New Salem.
1832	Lincoln makes his first run for public office but is not elected. Lincoln becomes a shopkeeper in partnership with a friend. A year later, the partner dies, and the shop goes bankrupt.
1833	Lincoln becomes a postmaster and impresses his neighbors by doing odd jobs until he has paid off all his and his late partner's debts. He becomes known as "Honest Abe."
1834	The Whig party is organized by Henry Clay of Kentucky and Daniel Webster of Massachusetts to oppose the policies of President Andrew Jackson. Lincoln runs again for the Illinois state legislature as a Whig and is elected for the first of four consecutive terms.
1837	Lincoln becomes a lawyer. He leaves New Salem and moves to nearby Springfield, the state capital, where he and another young lawyer, John Todd Stuart, open a successful law practice.
1839	In Springfield, Abraham Lincoln meets Mary Todd, the daughter of a wealthy Kentucky banker.
1840	William Henry Harrison becomes the first Whig to be elected president.
1841	Lincoln leaves the state legislature. Harrison dies after only a month in office and is succeeded by his Whig vice president, Southerner John Tyler.
1842	**November 4** — Abraham Lincoln and Mary Todd marry. The couple would have four sons, of whom only the eldest would survive into adulthood.

1843	Robert Todd Lincoln, Abraham and Mary Lincoln's first son, is born.
1846	Lincoln is elected to Congress as a Whig from Illinois. Edward Baker Lincoln, the Lincolns' second son, is born. The Mexican War breaks out. Lincoln, like most other Whigs, opposes the war as a Southern plot to gain new slave territories.
1848	The Mexican War ends. Under the Treaty of Guadalupe Hidalgo, the United States acquires the area that now makes up California, Nevada, Utah, and parts of Arizona, Colorado, New Mexico, and Wyoming.
1849	Lincoln returns to Springfield when his term in the House of Representatives expires.
1850	The Compromise of 1850 admits California as a free state and allows each territory from the newly annexed Mexican land to choose whether it will be slave or free, regardless of location. Four-year-old Edward Lincoln dies. The Lincolns' third son, William Wallace ("Willie") Lincoln, is born.
1852	*Uncle Tom's Cabin*, written by Harriet Beecher Stowe, creates a furor of antislavery and anti-South sentiment with its portrayal of life on a plantation.
1853	The last of the Lincolns' four sons, Thomas ("Tad") Lincoln, is born.
1854	The Kansas-Nebraska Act extends the Compromise of 1850 to all U.S. territories. The residents of these two new territories can now decide for themselves whether or not to allow slavery. The Republican party is formed.
1855	Lincoln runs for the U.S. Senate but withdraws before the election to give his support to another antislavery candidate.
1856	Lincoln joins the Republican party. Mexican War hero John C. Frémont becomes the first Republican candidate for president, but he loses the race to Democrat James Buchanan.
1858	Lincoln runs for a Senate seat against the popular Democrat Stephen A. Douglas, with whom he has the famous Lincoln-Douglas Debates. These seven debates take place between the months of August and October 1858 in Illinois. Lincoln loses the election but gains a national reputation as a speaker.
1860	**February** — Lincoln makes his first political appearance in the northeastern section of the United States when he addresses a rally at the Cooper Institute in New York. **May** — The Republicans choose Lincoln over leading candidate William H. Seward as their party's choice for the 1860 presidential election.

November — Lincoln wins a four-way race for the presidency, defeating Northern Democrat Stephen Douglas. His two other opponents are Southern Democrat John C. Breckinridge and Constitutional Union party candidate John Bell.

December 20 — South Carolina withdraws from the United States. It is soon followed by the states of Mississippi, Florida, Alabama, Georgia, Louisiana, and Texas.

1861 **February** — The seven rebel states form a new country, the Confederate States of America, electing Jefferson Davis as their president.

March 4 — Lincoln, aged fifty-two, is inaugurated as the sixteenth president of the United States.

April 12 — The Civil War begins at Fort Sumter in Charleston, South Carolina. During the next month, Virginia, Arkansas, Tennessee, and North Carolina join the Confederate States.

July 21 — Union armies invade the South and are turned back by Confederate general Thomas J. ("Stonewall") Jackson at the First Battle of Bull Run near Manassas Junction, Virginia.

November — A U.S. captain stops a British ship and arrests two Confederate diplomats aboard, bringing the United States to the brink of war with Britain.

1862 **February** — After falling sick with a fever, Willie Lincoln dies.

April — Union general Ulysses S. Grant defeats the Confederate forces at Shiloh Church near Pittsburg Landing, Tennessee.

August 31 — Confederate forces under General Robert E. Lee defeat Union forces at the Second Battle of Bull Run in Virginia.

September 17 — Union general George B. McClellan stops Lee near Antietam Creek at Sharpsburg, Maryland.

September 22 — Lincoln presents the Emancipation Proclamation, scheduled to take effect on January 1, 1863.

December — Confederate forces under General Lee defeat Union forces under General Ambrose E. Burnside at the Battle of Fredericksburg.

1863 **January 1** — The Emancipation Proclamation takes effect. All slaves in Confederate-controlled territory are thus freed.

May — At the Battle of Chancellorsville, in Virginia, Union forces are again defeated, but Confederate general Stonewall Jackson is mortally wounded and dies shortly afterward.

June — General Lee invades Pennsylvania.

July — Union general George C. Meade defeats Lee's Confederate forces at the Battle of Gettysburg in Pennsylvania. In the west, Vicksburg, Mississippi, falls to General Grant's men after a long siege.

November 19 — Lincoln delivers his now-famous Gettysburg Address at the dedication of the new military cemetery at Gettysburg, Pennsylvania.

1864 **March** — Lincoln names Grant the commander of the Union armies.

September — Union forces under General William Tecumseh Sherman capture Atlanta, Georgia.

November 8 — Lincoln is elected to a second term, defeating his Democratic challenger, General George C. McClellan.

November 16-December 22 — General William Tecumseh Sherman leads his famous "March to the Sea."

1865   **April 9** — Confederate general Robert E. Lee surrenders to Union general Ulysses S. Grant at Appomattox Court House, Virginia, marking the collapse of Confederate forces.

April 14 — Abraham Lincoln is shot by John Wilkes Booth while attending an evening performance of *Our American Cousin* at Ford's Theatre in Washington, D.C.

April 15 — Abraham Lincoln dies of his injuries at the age of fifty-six. He is later buried in Oak Ridge Cemetery in Springfield, Illinois.

December 18 — The Thirteenth Amendment, which abolishes slavery in all the states, becomes law.

1868   **July 28** — The Fourteenth Amendment is declared to be ratified. This amendment grants citizenship to all people born or naturalized in the United States but protects only adult males' right to vote.

1870   **March 30** — The Fifteenth Amendment is ratified. It forbids keeping U.S. citizens from voting on account of their "race, color, or previous condition of servitude," but it is ignored in many parts of the United States, mainly in the South, for decades.

Index

abolitionists 23, 24, 25, 36

Battles: of Antietam 41; of Chancellorsville 44; First Battle of Bull Run 34; of Fredericksburg 44; of Gettysburg 45; Second Battle of Bull Run 35-36, 40; of Shiloh 34-35

"black codes" 56

Booth, John Wilkes 53

Burnside, Ambrose E. 44

Cities and other places: Appomattox Court House, Virginia 50, 52; Atlanta, Georgia 49; Charleston Harbor, South Carolina 31; Fredericksburg, Virginia 44; Gettysburg, Pennsylvania 45, 47; Lexington, Kentucky 11; Little Pigeon Creek, Indiana 7, 9; New Salem, Illinois 8, 9, 10; Nolin Creek, Kentucky 7; Richmond, Virginia 35, 50; Sharpsburg, Maryland 41; Springfield, Illinois 10, 26, 55; Vicksburg, Mississippi 45, 46; Washington, D.C. 6, 30, 32, 36, 45, 50, 52, 55, 58

Civil War 31-50, 59

Compromise of 1850 24

Confederacy (Confederate States of America) 30, 31, 34, 36

cotton 13-14, 15

Davis, Jefferson 30, 34

Declaration of Independence 10, 23

Douglas, Stephen A. 28, 30

Emancipation Proclamation 5, 6, 37, 40-41, 43, 54

Everett, Edward 45

Ford's Theatre 52, 53

Fort Sumter 31

Gettysburg Address 45, 47, 58

Grant, Ulysses S. 35, 39, 44-45, 48, 50, 52

Industrial Revolution 13-14, 23

Jackson, Thomas J. ("Stonewall") 34

Johnson, Andrew 53

Johnston, Albert S. 35

Johnston, Sarah Bush (*see* Lincoln, Sarah Johnston)

Kansas-Nebraska Act 25, 26, 27, 28

King, Martin Luther, Jr. 58, 59

Ku Klux Klan 56, 58, 59

Lee, Robert E. 32, 40, 41, 45, 50, 52

Lincoln, Abraham: assassination of 52-54; birth and childhood of 7-9; children of 12, 38; early political and law careers of 9, 10-11, 12, 26, 27-28; election of as U.S. president 29, 50; in Illinois state legislature 10; marriage of 12

Lincoln, Mary Todd 11, 12, 37-38, 52

Lincoln, Nancy 7

Lincoln, Sarah (sister) 7

Lincoln, Sarah Johnston (stepmother) 7, 8, 26; children of 7

Lincoln, Thomas 7, 8, 9, 11

Louisiana Purchase 25

"March to the Sea" 49, 50, 51

McClellan, George B. 35, 41, 50

Missouri Compromise 24, 25

National Association for the Advancement of Colored People (NAACP) 58

Reconstruction Amendments 54, 55, 56

Sherman, William Tecumseh 48, 49, 50

slavery 14-27, 36-37, 38-39, 43, 54; banning of slave trade 17; life of a slave 18-21

Stowe, Harriet Beecher 25

Todd, Mary Ann (*see* Lincoln, Mary Todd)

United States: division of 13, 14, 21-25; history of 12, 13-14, 17-18; and secession of South 29-30; and surrender of South 50

United States Congress 14, 24, 25, 26, 54

United States Constitution 10

United States Supreme Court 54

White House 6, 29, 51

68